HWÆT!

Also by Peter Glassgold

HWÆT!

A Little Old English Anthology
of American Modernist Poetry

*Revised edition, translated and edited
by Peter Glassgold*

GREEN INTEGER
KØBENHAVN & LOS ANGELES
2012

GREEN INTEGER
Edited by Per Bregne
København / Los Angeles
Distributed in the United States by Consortium Book
Sales and Distribution/Perseus
Distributed in England and throughout Europe by
Turnaround Publisher Services
Unit 3, Olympia Trading Estate
Coburg Road, Wood Green, London N22 6TZ
44 (0)20 88293009
ON NET available through Green Integer
(323) 857-1115 / http://www.greeninteger.com

Green Integer
6022 Wilshire Boulevard, Suite 202C
Los Angeles, California 90036 USA

Series Design: Per Bregne
Book Design and Typography: Pablo Capra
Cover photograph: On Location Studios

LIBRARY OF CONGRESS IN PUBLICATION DATA
Peter Glassgold
Hwæt: A Little Old English Anthology of Modernist Poetry
ISBN: 978-1-933382-41-8
p. cm – Green Integer 201
I. Title II. Series III. Translator: Peter Glassgold
Green Integer books are published for Douglas Messerli
Printed in the United States of America on acid-free paper.

For Suzanne

Contents

Foreword to the Second Edition

It has been twenty-seven years since the first edition of *Hwæt!* appeared. From the start its reception hovered between cult book and conversation piece. Most reviewers enjoyed it immensely—and there were quite a number of reviews, even in the New York and Los Angeles *Times*. Almost predictably, though, Old English specialists were baffled at best and offended at worst by these patascholarly "back" translations. However, no mockery of their field was intended. On the contrary, for someone who at this writing has been reading Old English with great love and pleasure for some fifty years, I honor their work and could not have accomplished my own without it. But I cannot call a language absolutely dead unless there is no one alive who understands it. And if it is not absolutely dead, then why not explore ways of using it anew that might stir immediate interest in people who speak its contemporary descendant? Language-play is what makes our species every bit as much *homo ludens* as *homo sapiens*.

For this second edition I have added three poems: "Storm," an early Imagist work by H.D., and two recent haiku by Michael McClure. I have also made a couple of small corrections in the Old English and emended the notes slightly. Once again, I am deeply grateful to Douglas Messerli, who published the Ur-*Hwæt!* at Sun & Moon Press and suggested that I expand and revise it for Green Integer Books. Day by day, *maca hit niwe!*

Peter Glassgold

Foreword (1985)

"MAKE it new." Ezra Pound's watchword for modernism proclaimed the poets' discarding of the self-consciously "poetical." Free verse ought to be free from the bounds of traditional forms and language and the need of set classical allusions for meaning. Let the sense of the poem be carried purely in its words.

Theoretically, poems with such purity of language should be easily translatable. Could they even be translated back in linguistic time? I became curious to find how poems in the modernist mode, starting with Pound and William Carlos Williams and working up to American poets of the present day, might sound in the English of a thousand years ago.

The attempt at "back" translation is not without precedent. Starting with the seventeenth-century antiquarians who recovered the manuscripts that became the main body of existing Old English literature, scholarship has occasionally taken an ingenious turn, working on the whole with nursery rhymes and other such conservative forms. My own approach, however, is more in the spirit of Dada than Germanic philology, and what began part joke, part mad game, grew in the delighted response of friends.

The twenty-five poems gathered here in translation are, of course, not to be taken as a definitive collection. The selection is limited by my own taste, by the natural restrictions arising from translating into a nearly forgotten ancestral tongue with a rather small surviving vocabulary and a full system of declensions, and by the style and nationality of the poets. (For the latter considerations, accordingly, T. S. Eliot is not included, since I regard him more British than American.)

These translations, for the most part, do not draw on the Old English poetic tradition, which was highly stylized—it was never my intention to recreate modern poems in the ancient alliterative manner, perfectly intelligible to King Alfred's court. I have tried to use what it seems to me must have been words in everyday speech. Where such words were lacking in the historical record, I made them up: word-formation in Old English comes naturally. *Maca hit niwe.*

The preparation of a book of translations is never a private endeavor. I am especially grateful to Walter Hamady of The Perishable Press Limited, James Laughlin of New Directions, and Daniel Weissbort of *Modern Poetry in Translation* for their spontaneous offers to publish some of my efforts; to Richard Barnes, Kim Robert Stafford, and Brian Swann for their time, scholarship, and advice, which helped define my own purposes

14

and the limits of this collection. I would like to thank my friends and colleagues at New Directions for their happy encouragement over the years, and so many others who read these translations of mine with evident pleasure: Eileen Allman, John Allman, Carol Jane Bangs, Linda Georgianna, Daniel Javitch, Ann Laughlin, André Lefevere, Rika Lesser, John Ratti, Eliot Weinberger, and George Zournas.

Preparation of a book is one thing; actual publication is quite another. Toby Olson promoted it; Douglas Messerli published it, and for these things my words cannot express the gratitude I feel.

Peter Glassgold

A Note on the Title and a Few Words
About Spelling and Pronunciation

HWÆT! is the cry—usually rendered "lo!"—that opens such Old English poems as *The Dream of the Rood* and *Beowulf.* It can also mean "what," "who," and "quick."

The phonetic values of Old English letters seem to have been much the same as Latin. There were some special signs, of which only two are used here. The symbol *7* is the scribal equivalent of our own ampersand. The runic "thorn" (Þ, þ) represents the modern "th" combination, both voiced and unvoiced—as in "*th*is" and "*th*in." Þ was voiced between vowels and between a vowel and another voiced consonant. It was unvoiced in all other positions and when doubled. The letters *f* and *s* were likewise voiced (as in our *v* and *z*) or unvoiced.

R was trilled at the beginning of a word and otherwise sounded emphatically, as in Dutch and American Midwestern pronunciation.

The letters *c* and *g* had both a hard (*k, g*) and soft (*ch, y*) pronunciation, not readily determined, though modern forms often serve as guides. In any case, the soft manner is printed here as *ċ* and *ġ*. The combination *cg* was a voiced *ċ* (as in fu*dge*). *Sċ* was generally pronounced in a soft manner (*sh*ip). The occasional hard sound (as*k*, *sch*ool), once again, follows modern usage in the main.

H initially or in combination (*hw*, *hl*, *hr*) was always pronounced, and with the modern breathing sound. Otherwise, it was gutturalized, as in German or Scots.

In general, Latin or Italian usage seems the best approximation for vowels. The combination *æ* in Old English, however, was pronounced pl*ay* when long and *a*t when short. In dipthongs, the emphasis was on the first vowel.

Stress was generally on the root element or the first syllable if it was not a prefix, as in English today and all other Germanic languages.

POEMS

JOHN ALLMAN
CAVE PAINTINGS

A one-legged bird in profile, short of beak,
off balance. The lance in my abdomen
like a needle in the egg that is my body,
& one eye: I see the long antelopes that fly
on the opposite wall, a thumbprint of light,
your ocher eye. You are the humpbacked male,
rearing, your genitals hung too high & behind,
the soul of cat, the joints of wings in your jaws.
O if I could move, disengage the lance,
I would travel across, flutter behind you,
my eye would fill with blood & be afraid.
You would turn outward in darkness
& around, to face me, hornless & smooth,
we would place ourselves eye over eye.

But I am the blow to your hearing,
the bowl that will be made of your skull,
the eye-sockets of your enemy
rising in the midnight fire. I am the dream
of your skin hung from the leafless tree.

JOHN ALLMAN
SCRÆF-FÆHUNGA

Anfete bridd healfweardes, mid sċortum nebbe,
tealtod. Þæt spere on minre wambe
ġeliċ nædle on þæm æġe þe is min bodiġ,
7 an eage: iċ seo þa langan eolas þe fleogaþ
uppan þæm andweardan wealle, þumaspor leohtes,
þin ġeoloreade eage. Þu eart se hofereda wer,
wiþerċierrende, þinu ġecyndlimu hangod to heah 7
    behindan,
seo sawol of catte, þa ġefog feþrena on þinum
    ġeaflum.
La! ġif iċ meahte onstyrian, wiþteon þæt spere,
iċ wolde faran ofer, floterian behindan þe,
min eage sċolde fyllan mid blode 7 forhtian.
Þu woldest hweorfan utweardes on deorcnesse
7 ymbe, toweard me, hornleas 7 smeþe,
wit wolden stcllan uncere selfe eage ofer eagan.

Ac iċ eom se dynt to þinre hlyste,
se bolla þe biþ worht of þinum heafde,
þa eagehringas þines feondes
risende midnihtes on þæm fyre. Iċ eom þæt swefn
of þinre hyde uppan þæm leafleasan treowe
    ġehangen.

MEDITATION 4

if a sick man enters a house the members of the
household are all more or less susceptible to his
disease   and it will spread by contact from the
infected to the uninfected   and each infected will
run the course of his sickness and recover or die of
his sickness   and his chances to recover or die of
his sickness will vary from day to day in the course
of his sickness   and his chances of conveying his
sickness to the uninfected will vary from day to day
       as the sickness spreads there will be fewer and
fewer members who may become infected   one
day the sickness will come to an end

DAVID ANTIN
SMEANG IV

ġif seoc mann ingæþ hus þa hiwan beoþ ma
oþþe læs opene to his onflyġe   and he sprædþ
þurh hrinenesse of þæm onġefolgenum to þæm
unonġefolgenum   and ælċ onġefolgen iernþ his
seocnesse ryne and godaþ oþþe swilt of his seocnesse
    and his wyrdġesċeapu to godienne oþþe
sweltenne wrixlaþ dæġhwamliċe on his seocnesse
ryne   and his wyrdġesċeapu to berenne his
seocnesse to þæm unonġefolgenum wrixlaþ
dæġhwamliċe   þa hwile þe seo seocnes sprædþ
þær beon feawran and feawran hiwan þa þe moton
onġefolgene weorþan   sume dæġ seo seocnes
endaþ

JOHN BERRYMAN
DREAM SONG 315

Behind me twice her necessary knight
she comes like one of Spenser's ladies
on a white palfrey
and it is cold & full dark in the valley,
though I haven't seen a dragon for days, & faint
        moonlight
gives my horse footing till dawn.

My lady is all in green, for innocence
I am in black, a terror to my foes
who are numerous & strong.
I haven't lost a battle yet but I am tense
for the first losing. I wipe blood from my nose
and raise up my voice in song.

Hard lies the road behind, hard that ahead
but we are armed & armoured & we trust
entirely one another.
We have beaten down the foulest of them, lust,
and we pace on in peace, like sister & brother,
doing that to which we were bred.

JOHN BERRYMAN
SWEFNSANG CCCXV

Behindan me twa hiere niedbehofan cempan
heo cymþ ġeliċ Spenseres hlæfdiġena anre
uppan blancan
and hit is ċeald 7 full deorc on þæm dæle,
þeah iċ ne seah dracan for dagum, 7 dimm
    monanleoht
ġiefþ minum meare fæstne fot oþ dæġred.

Minu hlæfdiġe is eall on grene, for unsċeþþiġnesse
iċ eom on blæċe, gryre to minum ġcfam
þa þe sind maniġe 7 strange.
Iċ ne forleas ġefeoht þa ġiet þeah iċ stific
for þæm forman lyre. Iċ wipie blod of minre nosa
and ahebbe up mine stefne on sange.

Heard liþ seo rad behindan, heard seo foran
ac wit sind ġewæpnod 7 ġesierwed 7 wit treowiaþ
eallunga ælċum oþrum.
Wit beoton adune hiera þone fulostan, lust,
and wit forþgaþ on friþe, ġeliċ sweostor 7 breþer,
donde þæt wit acenned wæron þærto.

ROBERT DUNCAN
OFTEN I AM PERMITTED TO RETURN TO A MEADOW

as if it were a scene made-up by the mind,
that is not mine, but is a made place,

that is mine, it is so near to the heart,
an eternal pasture folded in all thought
so that there is a hall therein

that is a made place, created by light
wherefrom the shadows that are forms fall.

Wherefrom fall all architectures I am
I say are likenesses of the First Beloved
whose flowers are flames lit to the Lady.

She it is Queen Under The Hill
whose hosts are a disturbance of words within words
that is a field folded.

It is only a dream of the grass blowing
east against the source of the sun
in an hour before the sun's going down

ROBERT DUNCAN
OFT IĊ MOT EFTĊIERRAN TO SUMRE MÆDWE

swa heo wære wafung macod mid mode,
þe nis min, bute is macod stow,

þe is min, heo is swa neah to þære heortan,
eċe edisċ fealden on eallum ġeþohte
swa þæt þær is heall þærinne

þe is macod stow, sċapen mid leohte
hwanon þa scadwa þe sind hiw feallaþ.

Hwanon feallaþ ealla ġetimbrunga iċ eom
iċ secge sind ġeliċnessa of þæm Ærestan Leofe
þæs þe blostmas sind liegas inliehted to þære
     Hlæfdiġan.

Heo selfu biþ Cwen Under Þæm Hylle
þære þe ġedryhta sind drefung of wordum innan
     wordum
þe is feld fealden.

Hit is efne swefn of þæm græse blowendum
east toġeanes þære sunnan frumstowe
anre tide ær þære sunnan niþerstiġe

whose secret we see in a children's game
of ring a round of roses told.

Often I am permitted to return to a meadow
as if it were a given property of the mind
that certain bounds hold against chaos,

that is a place of first permission,
everlasting omen of what is.

þæs þe dieġelnesse we seoþ on ċildra gamene
of hringe ymb þa rosan teald.

Oft iċ mot eftċierran to sumre mædwe
swa heo wære staþolæht of þæm mode
þe fæsta mearca healdaþ wiþ dwolman,

þe is stow of ærestan leafe,
eċe wyrdtacen of þæm þe is.

H.D.
STORM

You crash over the trees,
you crack the live branch—
the branch is white,
the green crushed,
each leaf is rent like split wood.

You burden the trees
with black drops,
you swirl and crash—
you have broken off a weighted leaf
in the wind,
it is hurled out,
whirls up and sinks,
a green stone.

H.D.
STORM

Þu bricst ofer þa treowu,
þu clyfst þone cwican boga—
se bog is hwit,
þæt grene gebriesed,
ælċ leaf is rended ġeliċ snidenan wuda.

Þu hlatst þa treowu
mid blæcum dropum,
þu hwærfiast and bricst—
þu tobrægde gehefod leaf
in winde, hit is aworpen,
upwielþ and sincþ,
an grene stan.

JAMES LAUGHLIN
IT DOES ME GOOD

to bow my body to the ground
when the emperor passes I am

one of the gardeners at the
palace but I have never seen

his face when he walks in the
garden he is preceded by boys

who ring little bells and I
bow myself down when I hear

the bells approaching though
they say that the emperor is

very kind and not easily of—
fended he might smile at me

if I look up or even speak
to me but I believe that the

emperor rules by my humility
it is my humility that rules.

JAMES LAUGHLIN
HIT DEÞ ME TO GODE

to bugenne min bodiġ to þæm grunde
þaþa se casere oferfærþ iċ eom

ortġeardwearda an æt þæm
caserhame ac iċ ne ġeseah næfre

his ansien þaþa he gæþ on þæm
ortġearde he is foregan be ġeonglingum

þa þe hringaþ lytla bellan and iċ
buge me selfne ofdune þaþa iċ hiere

þa bellan nealæċende þæh-þe
hie secgaþ þæt se casere sie

swiþe milde and na eaþe ne ġe-
bolġen he moste hliehhan on me

ġif iċ locie up oþþe furþum sprecan
to me ac iċ ġeliefe þæt se

casere ricsaþ be minre eaþmodnesse
min eaþmodnes self heo ricsaþ.

DENISE LEVERTOV
ILLUSTRIOUS ANCESTORS

The Rav
of Northern White Russia declined,
in his youth, to learn the
language of birds, because
the extraneous did not interest him; nevertheless
when he grew old it was found
he understood them anyway, having
listened well, and as it is said, 'prayed
      with the bench and the floor.' He used
what was at hand—as did
Angel Jones of Mold, whose meditations
were sewn into coats and britches.
      Well, I would like to make,
thinking some line still taut between me and them,
poems direct as what the birds said,
hard as a floor, sound as a bench,
mysterious as the silence when the tailor
would pause with his needle in the air.

DENISE LEVERTOV
MÆRE FOREGENGAN

Se Rabbi
of Norþerne Hwitre Russie nolde,
on his ġeogoþe, to leornienne þæt
fugliscan ġereord, for þæm þe
se uterra ne beheold him; swaþeah
þaþa he wearþ eald man funde
he understod hie æġhwæs,
hlysnende wel, and swa man sæġþ, 'gebiddende
            mid þære benċe and þære flora.' He breac
swa hwæs swa wæs to handa—swa dyde
Enġel Jones of Molde, þæs smeanga
siwoda wæron on haman and breċ.
            Wel, hit wolde licaþ me to sċiepenne,
þenċende sumu line þa ġiet togen betweon me and
      him,
sċopleoþ on ġerihte swaswa hwæt þa fuglas sæġdon,
heard swaswa flora, ġesund swaswa benċe,
ġerynelicu swaswa þære stilnesse þaþa se seamere
wolde blinnan mid his nædle on þære lyfte.

ROBERT LOWELL
WATER

It was a Maine lobster town—
each morning boatloads of hands
pushed off for granite
quarries on the islands,

and left dozens of bleak
white frame houses stuck
like oyster shells
on a hill of rock,

and below us, the sea lapped
the raw little match-stick
mazes of weir,
where the fish for bait were trapped.

Remember? We sat on a slab of rock.
From this distance in time,
it seems the color
of iris, rotting and turning purpler,

but it was only
the usual gray rock
turning the usual green
when drenched by the sea.

ROBERT LOWELL
WÆTER

Hit was sum Maine loppestretun—
ælċe morne bathlæstas of mannum
sċufonut to stan-
ġedelfum on þæm ieġlandum,

and læfdon twelfeald blacra
hwitra ġetimbrodra husa sticodu
ġeliċ ostresċiellum
ofer hylle of clude,

and niþer unc, se sæ lapode
þa bæran lytlan sticcaliċan
ġewindu of sumum were,
hwær þa fisċas to æse wæron grinode.

Ahne ġemanst? Wit sæton uppan smeþum stanstyċċe.
Fram þys feorr on timan,
me þynċþ hit þæs hiwes
sċire blostmena, rotiende and weorþende hæwenra,

ac hit wæs efne
se ġewuna græġa stan
weorþende þæt ġewuna grene
þaþa awasċed fram þæm sæ.

37

The sea drenched the rock
at our feet all day,
and kept tearing away
flake after flake.

One night you dreamed
you were a mermaid clinging to a wharf-pile,
and trying to pull
off the barnacles with your hands.

We wished our two souls
might return like gulls
to the rock. In the end,
the water was too cold for us.

Se sæ awasċede þone stan
æt uncerum fotum ealne dæġ,
and wolde ateran onweġ
styċċe æfter styċċe.

Sumre nihte þu swefnodest
þu wære meremæġden clifiende to þæm hwearf-pile
and cunniende to pullienne
of þa muscellan mid þinum handum.

Wit wysċton uncera sawla
mosten hweorfan ġeliċ mæwum
to þæm stane. In ende,
þæt wæter wæs to ċeald for unc.

MICHAEL MCCLURE
TWO HAIKU

THE BIG
YELLOW
LEAF
S
P
I
N
S
through
the silver
down
pour.
—Smacks
my

wind
shield

LOOK THERE
'S A RAB
IT
No,
it's
maple leaves

MICHAEL McCLURE
TWO HAIKU

ÞÆT MICLA
GEOLWA
LEAF
T
Y
R
N
E
Þ
þurh
þone silfran
regen
storm.
—Smitt
mine

wind
scield

LOCA ÞÆR
IS AN HA
RA
Ne,
hit is
mapulleaf

blowing
down
a
drive
way

blawende
ofdune
anne
gedrif
weg.

MARIANNE MOORE
POETRY

I, too, dislike it.
    Reading it, however, with a perfect contempt
                      for it, one discovers in
    it, after all, a place for the genuine.

MARIANNE MOORE
LEOÞWEORC

Iċ, eac, hatie hit.
   Rædende hit, hwæþere, mid fullfremedre
      forhogodnesse
                     for him, man onfint on
   him, æfter ealle, sume stowe for þæm ġecyndliċe.

MARIANNE MOORE
TO A STEAM ROLLER

The illustration
is nothing to you without the application.
    You lack half wit. You crush all the particles down
        into close conformity, and then walk back and
            forth

                                    on them.

Sparkling chips of rock
are crushed down to the level of the parent block.
    Were not "impersonal judgment in aesthetic
        matters, a metaphysical impossibility," you

might fairly achieve
it. As for butterflies, I can hardly conceive
    of one's attending upon you, but to question
        the congruence of the complement is vain, if it
            exists.

MARIANNE MOORE
TO ANUM STEAMTREDERE

Seo sweotolung
is nanþing to þe butan þære dæde.
   Þu wanabist healfes wittes. Þu brytest eall þara
      styċċa ofdune
      on nearwe anfealdnesse, and þa gæst onbæc and
        forþ

                        ofer hie.

Spearciende brycas stana
weorþaþ ġebryted ofdune to þære grundstowe þæs
      cennendes cludes.
   Ġif nære "unagen dom be andġietsumum
      intingum, uþwitalicu unmihtnes" þu

mihte æġhwæs don
hine. Be buterfleogum, iċ mæġ uneaþe beþenċan
   hiera an þeġniende þe, ac to ascienne
      þa ġerisnesse þære gefyllednesse is idel, ġif heo
        stande.

MARIANNE MOORE
O TO BE A DRAGON

    If I, like Solomon,...
    could have my wish—

  my wish...O to be a dragon,
a symbol of the power of Heaven—of silkworm
size or immense; at times invisible.
  Felicitous phenomenon!

MARIANNE MOORE
LA TO WEORÞENNE DRACA

Ġif iċ, swa Salomon,...
mihte habban min ġewill—

min ġewill...la to weorþenne draca,
tacn þæs Heofonmæġnes—seolcwyrmes
ġemet oþþe unmæte; hwilum unġesiene.
Eadiġ wundor!

TOBY OLSON
THE SPOT

Who makes of his wife a goddess, is subject
to certain depression
     thinks he's a king
or trash unworthy

to possess her even
live in the same house
with her.

   either way her faults
pierce his groin like needles
also he walks around with a sick head.

Who loves her and then
seeks other women
faultless & perfect smelling
and longs for the nectar, he *is* trash
or a false king on his property.

He who loves her truly
however, will kiss a rash on her body
take in the smell of her breath in the morning—

TOBY OLSON
SE SPLOTT

Swa hwa swa macaþ of his hlæfdiġan gydenne, biþ
    open
to ġewissre sorgċeare
    þencþ is cyning
oþþe ġeswæpa unwierþa

to healdenne hie efne
wunienne on þæm ilcan huse
mid hiere.

    æġhwæþre wisan hiere wammas
stingaþ his lendenu ġeliċ nædlum
eac he ymbwandraþ mid seocum heafde.

Swa hwa swa lufaþ hie and þa
secþ oþre wifmenn
wamlease 7 ġestenċe
and langaþ him æfter þæm huniġteare, he *biþ*
    ġeswæpa
oþþe leas cyning ofer his æhte.

Swa hwa swa lufaþ hie soþliċe
swaþeah, wille cyssan bleġene uppan hiere bodiġe
inþicgan þone stenċ hiera æþmes on morgentide—

seeing her face in the textures of concrete walls
in the bellies of other women
He discovers his real value
and finds his spot.

   ġesiende hiera ansiene on þæm hiwum
     weallweorca
    on þære wambum oþra wifmanna
He onfint his soþ weorþ
and fint his splott.

GEORGE OPPEN
BOY'S ROOM

A friend saw the rooms
Of Keats and Shelley
At the lake, and saw 'they were just
Boys' rooms' and was moved

By that. And indeed a poet's room
Is a boy's room
And I suppose that women know it.

Perhaps the unbeautiful banker
Is exciting to a woman, a man
Not a boy gasping
For breath over a girl's body.

GEORGE OPPEN
ĠEONGLINGES BUR

Sum freond seah þa buras
Keatses and Shelleyes
Æt þæm mere, and seah 'hie wæron efne
Ġeonglinga buras' and wæs onstyred

Be þæm. And huru sċopes bur
Biþ ġeonglinges bur
And iċ wene þæt wifmenn cnawaþ hit.

Wenunga se unfæġera mynetere
Is onhætende to wifmenn, mann
Na ġeongling pyffende
For æþme ofer mæġdenċildes bodiġe.

EZRA POUND
A GIRL

The tree has entered my hands,
The sap has ascended my arms,
The tree has grown in my breast—
Downward,
The branches grow out of me, like arms.

Tree you are,
Moss you are,
You are violets with wind above them.
A child—*so* high—you are,
And all this is folly to the world.

EZRA POUND
MǼĠDENĊILD

Þæt treow ġeong binnan minre handum,
Þæt sæp astag mine earmas,
Þæt treow greow innan min breost—
Niþerweard,
Þa bogas growaþ of me, ġeliċ earmum.

Treow þu eart,
Meos þu eart,
Þu eart hæwene blostmas mid wind ufan him.
Cild—*swa* heah—þu eart,
And eall þis is dysiġ þære worulde.

EZRA POUND
IN A STATION OF THE METRO

The apparition of these faces in the crowd;
Petals on a wet, black bough.

EZRA POUND
ON TILLE OF ÞÆM UNDERWEĠE

Seo ætiewednes of þissum hleorum on þære drafe;
Blostmabladu on watum, blacum boge.

EZRA POUND
THE RIVER-MERCHANT'S WIFE:
A LETTER

While my hair was still cut straight across my
    forehead
I played about the front gate, pulling flowers.
You came by on bamboo stilts, playing horse,
You walked about my seat, playing with blue plums.
And we went on living in the village of Chōkan:
Two small people, without dislike or suspicion.

At fourteen I married My Lord you.
I never laughed, being bashful.
Lowering my head, I looked at the wall.
Called to, a thousand times, I never looked back.

At fifteen I stopped scowling,
I desired my dust to be mingled with yours
Forever and forever and forever.
Why should I climb the look out?

At sixteen you departed,
You went into far Ku-tō-en, by the river of swirling
    eddies,

EZRA POUND
WIF ÞÆS STREAM-MANGERES:
AN ĠEWRIT

Þa-hwile-þe min hær wæs þa ġiet efesod ofer minum
    forheafode
Iċ plegode ymb þæt fore ġeat, pulliende blostman.
Þu com neah uppan bambusum palum, pleġiende
    hors,
Þu eodest ymb min sess, pleġiende mid hæwene
    pluman.
And we alifdon on þaem tune Ċiōkan:
Twa lytlu folc, wiþutan mislicunge oþþe
    mistruwunge.

Æt feowertiene iċ weddode Minne Hlaford þe.
Iċ ne hloh næfre, wesende sċeoh.
Niþerhieldende min heafod, iċ locode on þone weall.
Clipod, an þusend siþa, iċ ne locode underbæc næfre.

Æt fiftiene iċ blann fram gramum andwlitan,
Iċ willode min dust sie menġed mid urum
Æfre and æfre and æfre.
Hwy scolde iċ climman þone weardsetl?

Æt siextiene þu fiersode,
Þu eodest into feorr Ku-tō-en, be þæm streame of
    hwyrfe-polum,

61

And you have been gone five months.
The monkeys make sorrowful noise overhead.
You dragged your feet when you went out.
By the gate now, the moss is grown, the different
    mosses,
Too deep to clear them away!
The leaves fall early this autumn, in wind.
The paired butterflies are already yellow with August
Over the grass in the West garden;
They hurt me. I grow older.
If you are coming down through the narrows of the
    river Kiang
Please let me know beforehand,
And I will come out to meet you
                As far as Chō-fū-Sa

By Rihaku (Li T'ai Po)

And nu þu eart afaren fif monaþ.
Þa apan maciaþ sorgfulle ġehlyd ufan.
Þu droh eowere fet þaþa þu eode ute.
Be þæm ġeate nu, se meos is growen, þa
    maniġfealdan meosas,
To deope hiera to sċirenne!
Þa leaf fielaþ ærliċe þys hærfeste, on winde.
Þa twinnan buterfleogan beoþ ær nu ġeolwod fram
    Auguste
Ofer þæm gærse on þæm Westan ortġearde;
Hie hefiġiaþ me; iċ growe ieldre.
Ġif þu cume ofdune þurh þa nearo þæs streames
    Kianges,
Iċ bidde þe þæt þu cyþe me beforan,
And iċ wille cuman ut to metenne þe
              Swa feorr swa Ciō-fū-Sa.

Be Rihaku (Li T'ai Po)

JOHN RATTI
ALBUM

The big black bear
cuddled next to the hunter
in the white snow
is dead;
so are the bucks,
nestled like kittens
in the tall weeds,
their antlers dry as twigs;
so are the trout,
mouths hooked together
and displayed
against a well-grained
wood plank;
so is the black-haired
younger brother
who hitched up his pants
and balanced on a log raft
with the men from the mill;
so is his fine bay horse,
hitched to a trim little rig
and staring straight ahead
into the sepia field
where he was foaled
and later buried.

JOHN RATTI
ĠEMYNDBOC

Se miċla blæca bera
sett niehst þæm huntan
on þæm hwitan snawe
is dead;
swa sind þa buccas,
leġde ġeliċ cytelingum
on þæm heam weodum,
hiera hornas dryġe swa twigu;
swa sind þa truht,
muþas samodfæste mid hocum
and ætiewede
onġean cneowehtum
wuda borde;
swa is se blæcfeaxeda
ġingra broþor
se þe teah upp his breċ
and efenweġen ofer treowa fleot
mid þæm mannum of þæm mylne;
swa is his god brun mearh,
þe dræġþ trumne lytelne wæġn
and staraþ rihte forþ
into þæm græġan felde
hwær he wæs folod
and siþra byrġed.

KENNETH REXROTH
DELIA REXROTH

California rolls into
Sleepy summer, and the air
Is full of the bitter sweet
Smoke of the grass fires burning
On the San Francisco hills.
Flesh burns so, and the pyramids
Likewise, and the burning stars.
Tired tonight, in a city
Of parvenus, in the inhuman
West, in the most blood drenched year,
I took down a book of poems
That you used to like, that you
Used to sing to music I
Never found anywhere again—
Michael Field's book, *Long Ago*.
Indeed it's long ago now—
Your bronze hair and svelte body.
I guess you were a fierce lover,
A wild wife, an animal
Mother. And now life has cost
Me more years, though much less pain,
Than you had to pay for it.
And I have bought back, for and from

KENNETH REXROTH
DELIA REXROÞ

California wielcþ on
Slæpiġne sumor, and seo lyft
Is full þæs biteran swetan
Smocan of þæm gærsfyrum biernendum
Ofer þa San Franciscan hyllas.
Flæsċ biernþ swa, and þa enta ġeweorc
Geliċe, and þa biernendan steorran.
Teorod toniht, on byriġ
Becumendra manna, on þæm unmenniscum
Westdæle, on þæm mæst bloddrenċedan ġeare,
Iċ tac ofune boc of sċopleoþum
þe licode þe æror, þe þu
Wunode singan mid gliwe iċ ne
Næfre funde eft nahwær—
Michael Fieldes boc, *Lange Agan*.
Huru hit is lange agan nu—
Þin ære hær and swancore bodiġ.
Iċ telle þu wære strangu lufestre,
Wilde wif, nietenlicu
Modor. And nu lif stod
Me maran ġear, þeah miċle læsse sar,
Þonne þu scolde ġieldan for him.
And iċ bohte onbæc, for and of

Myself, these poems and paintings,
Carved from the protesting bone,
The precious consequences
Of your torn and distraught life.

Me selfum, þas sċopleoþ and fæhunga,
Corfen of uncweþendum bane,
Þa dieran wyrde
Of þinum torenan and unstillan life.

JEROME ROTHENBERG

A POEM IN YELLOW AFTER TRISTAN TZARA

angel slide your hand
into my basket   eat my yellow fruit
my eye is craving it
my yellow tires screech
o dizzy human heart
my yellow dingdong

JEROME ROTHENBERG
SĊOPLEOÞ ON ĠEOLONESSE ÆFTER TRISTANE TZARAN

enġel slid þine hand
on mine sacc⠀⠀⠀et minne ġeolwan wæstm
min eage langaþ hit
min ġeolwan hweol scralletaþ
la dysiġe mennisċe heorte
min ġeolwa hringhrang

GARY SNYDER
BY FRAZIER CREEK FALLS

Standing up on lifted, folded rock
looking out and down—

The creek falls to a far valley
hills beyond that
facing, half-forested, dry
—clear sky
strong wind in the
stiff glittering needle clusters
of the pine—their brown
round trunk bodies
straight, still;
rustling trembling limbs and twigs

listen.

This living flowing land
is all there is, forever

We *are* it
it sings through us—

We could live on this Earth
without clothes or tools!

GARY SNYDER
BE FRAZIERES BROCES WÆTERĠEFEALLE

Standende uppe ofer hafenum, fealdenum stanrocce
lociende ut and ofdune—

Se broc fielþ to sumum feorrum dæle
hyllas beġeondan þæm
toweard, healf-wudufæstede, dryġe
—leohtre lyfte
strang wind on þæm
stifan glisniendan nædlclystrum
þara pintreowa—hiera brunu
sincwcaltu stemn-bodiġ
rihtu, stillu;
swogendu cwaciendu limu and twigu

hlyste.

Þis libbende flowende land
is eall þæt is, æfre

We *beoþ* hit
hit singþ þurh us—

We meahton libban ofter þisse Eorþe
claþa oþþe tola leas!

WALLACE STEVENS
ANECDOTE OF THE JAR

I placed a jar in Tennessee,
And round it was, upon a hill.
It made the slovenly wilderness
Surround that hill.

The wilderness rose up to it,
And sprawled around, no longer wild.
The jar was round upon the ground
And tall and of a port in air.

It took dominion everywhere.
The jar was gray and bare.
It did not give of bird or bush,
Like nothing else in Tennessee.

WALLACE STEVENS
ÞÆS CROCCES SPELL

Ic sette crocc on Tennessee,
And sinewealt he wæs, uppan hylle.
He macode þa receleasan wildeornesse
Ymbhringan þone hyll.

Wildeornes aras up þærto,
And spreawolde ymbutan, na leng wildu.
Se crocc wæs sinewealt uppan þæm grunde
And lang and gemete on lyfte.

He toc geweald æghwær.
Se crocc wæs græg and bær.
He ne geaf nænigne bridd ne scrybbe,
Gelic nanþinge elles on Tennessee.

WALLACE STEVENS
THE GLASS OF WATER

That the glass would melt in heat,
That the water would freeze in cold,
Shows that this object is merely a state,
One of many, between two poles. So,
In the metaphysical, there are these poles.

Here in the centre stands the glass. Light
Is the lion that comes down to drink. There
And in that state, the glass is a pool.
Ruddy are his eyes and ruddy are his claws
When light comes down to wet his frothy jaws

And in the water winding weeds move round.
And there and in another state—the refractions,
The *metaphysica*, the plastic parts of poems
Crash in the mind—But, fat Jocundus, worrying
About what stands here in the centre, not the glass,

But in the centre of our lives, this time, this day,
It is a state, this spring among the politicians
Playing cards. In a village of the indigenes,
One would have still to discover. Among the dogs
        and dung,
One would continue to contend with one's ideas.

WALLACE STEVENS
ÞÆT GLÆSFÆT OF WÆTERE

Þæt þæt glæsfæt wolde meltan on hate,
Þæt þæt wæter wolde freosan on ċealde,
Sweotolaþ þæt þis þing is anliċe sum staþol,
Maniġra an, betweonan twæm utemestum. Swa,
On þæm ġeondcyndliċum, þær sind þas utemestan.

Her on middan stent þæt glæsfæt. Leoht
Is se leo þe cymþ ofdune to drincenne. Þær
And on þæm staþole, þæt glæsfæt is pol.
Rudiġu sind his eagan and rudiġan sind his clawa
Þaþa leoht cymþ ofdune to wætenne his famiġan
    ċeaflas

And on þæm wætere windendu weod ymbhwierfaþ.
And þær and on oþrum staþole—þa brytsenna,
Þa *metaphysica*, þa ġesċeapbæran partas of leoþum
Hlynsiaþ on þæm mode—Ac, fætt Jocundus, cariende
Be hwæm stent her on middan, ne þæm glæsfæte,

Bute on middan of urum lifum, þys timan, þys dæġe,
Hit is sum staþol, þes spryng onġemang þæm
    burgwealdum
Þe pleġiaþ cartan. On wiċe þara inborenra,
Man sċolde nu ġiet ontfindan. Onġemang þæm
    hundum and dunge,
Man sċolde ġesingalian to flitenne wiþ manes
    ġeþeahtu.

WALLACE STEVENS
THE MOTIVE FOR METAPHOR

You like it under the trees in autumn,
Because everything is half dead.
The wind moves like a cripple among the leaves
And repeats words without meaning.

In the same way, you were happy in spring.
With the half colors of quarter-things,
The slightly brighter sky, the melting clouds,
The single bird, the obscure moon—

The obscure moon lighting an obscure world
Of things that would never be quite expressed,
Where you yourself were never quite yourself
And did not want nor have to be,

Desiring the exhilarations of changes:
The motive for metaphor, shrinking from
The weight of primary noon,
The A B C of being,

The ruddy temper, the hammer
Of red and blue, the hard sound—
Steel against intimation—the sharp flash,
The vital, arrogant, fatal, dominant X.

WALLACE STEVENS
SE INTINGA FOR ĠEONDLÆDUNGE

Hit licaþ þe under þæm treowum on hærfeste,
For þæm þe eall is healfe dead.
Se wind styraþ ġeliċ creople onġemang þæm leafum
And edlæsteþ word wiþutan ġetacnunge.

Swa ilce, þu wære bliþe on lenctne,
Mid þæm healfan hiwum feorþungþinga,
Þæm heofone beorhtran lyt, þæm meltendum
    wolcnum,
Þæm syndriġan bridde, þæm dyrnan monan —

Se dyrna mona liehtende dyrne woruldc
Of þingum þe wolde næfre ealles sweotolod weorþan,
Hwær þu self wære næfre ealles þu self
And nolde ne sċolde beon,

Wilniende þara glædnessa of ġewrixlum:
Se intinga for ġeondlædunge, sċrincende fram
Þæm wihte of forman mid-dæġtide,
Þæm abecede of beonde,

Þære rudiġan stielednesse, þæm hamore
Reades and hæwenes, þæm heardan hlemme —
Stiele wiþ cuþnesse—þære sċearpan glitenunge,
Þæm lifliċan, hean, deadliċan, wealdendan X.

WILLIAM CARLOS WILLIAMS
THE WIDOW'S LAMENT IN SPRINGTIME

Sorrow is my own yard
where the new grass
flames as it has flamed
often before but not
with the cold fire
that closes round me this year.
Thirtyfive years
I lived with my husband.
The plumtree is white today
with masses of flowers.
Masses of flowers
load the cherry branches
and color some bushes
yellow and some red
but the grief in my heart
is stronger than they
for though they were my joy
formerly, today I notice them
and turn away forgetting.
Today my son told me
that in the meadows,
at the edge of the heavy woods
in the distance, he saw
trees of white flowers.

WILLIAM CARLOS WILLIAMS
ÞÆRE WUDEWAN SORGLEOÞ ON LENCTNE

Sorg is min agen ġeard
hwær þæt niwe gærs
birnþ swaswa hit wolde biernan
oft foran ac ne
mid þæm ċealdan fyre
þe ymbliþ me þys ġeare.
Fif and þritiġ ġearum
iċ lifde mid minum mannan.
Þæt plum-treow is hwite todæġ
mid meniġum of blostmum.
Meniġa of blostmum
hlæstaþ þa ċirsbogas
and hiwiaþ sume sċrybbe
ġeolwe and sume reade
ac seo gnorgnung on minre heortan
is strengre þonne hie
for þæh-þe hie wæron min bliss
ær, todæġ iċ onġiette hie
and turne onweġ forġietende.
Todæġ min sunu tealde me
þæt on þæm mædum,
æt þære ecge þara hefiġra wuda
feorran, he seah
treow hwitra blostmena.

I feel that I would like
to go there
and fall into those flowers
and sink into the marsh near them.

Iċ felþ þæt hit wolde licaþ me
to farenne þær
and to feallenne on þas blostman
and to sincenne on þone mersċ neah him.

WILLIAM CARLOS WILLIAMS
THE RED WHEELBARROW

so much depends
upon

a red wheel
barrow

glazed with rain
water

beside the white
chickens.

WILLIAM CARLOS WILLIAMS
SEO READE HWEOLBEARWE

swa miċel hangaþ
on

readre hweol
bearwan

glasiġre of reġen
wætere

be sidan þæm hwitan
ċycenum.

WILLIAM CARLOS WILLIAMS
THIS IS JUST TO SAY

I have eaten
the plums
that were in
the icebox

and which
you were probably
saving
for breakfast

Forgive me
they were delicious
so sweet
and so cold

WILLIAM CARLOS WILLIAMS
PYS IS EFNE TO SECGENNE

Iċ æt
þa pluman
þe wæron on
þære isċieste

and þe
þu eallmæst cuþliċe
hordodest
for morgenmete

Forġief me
hie wæron smæccliċe
swa swete
and swa ċealde

Notes

John Allman: Cave Paintings

SCRÆF-FÆHUNGA: combining *scræf*, "cave," and the plural *fæhunga*, derived from *fæhan*, to "paint." **An-fete**: "one-footed." **healfweardes**: **in profile**: that is, "to the side." **tealtod**: **off balance**: literally, "unsteadied," from *tealtian*, akin to the modern "tilt." **eolas**: plural of *eolh*, "elk." The word "antelope," derived from medieval Greek, is of uncertain meaning, **ġeoloreade**: **ocher**: "yellow-red." **se hoferede wer**: **the humpbacked male**: *hofereda* from *hofer*, "hump"; *wer*, "man," that is, one of the male sex. **þa ġefog feþrena on þinum ġeaflum**: **the joints of wings in your jaws**: a literal translation. The words "joint," "wing," "jaw" derive from Middle English. **wiþteon**: "withdraw." **wit**: "we two." The OE pronoun system has dual as well as singular and plural forms. **uncere selfe**: "our two selfs." Again, the dual number. **þa eagehringas þines feondes**: "the eye-rings of your enemy [thy fiend's]."

David Antin: meditation 4

smeang: **meditation**: from *smeagan*, to "penetrate," "reflect," "meditate." **þa hiwan**: "the household members."

89

A single household member, *hiwa*, belongs to a *hiwen* (family), a *hiwræden* (cloister), or *husræden* (secular household). **onflyġe**: "[infectious] disease," from *fleogan*, to "fly." **þurh hrinenesse**: **by contact**: derived from *hrinan*, to "touch." **of þæm onġefolgenum to þæm unonġefolgenum**: **from the infected to the uninfected**: cf. *onflyġe*, above. **iernþ his seocnesse ryne**: "runs his sickness's run." **godaþ**: **recover**: that is, get better, literally, "get good." **swilt**: **die**: The verb *sweltan* is akin to "swelter." **wyrdġesċeapu**: **chances**: "fate-shapes." **wrixlaþ dæġhwamliċe**: "change daily."

John Berryman: Dream Song 315
hiere niedbehofan cempan: "her need-behooved champion." In OE, knight (*cniht*) generally has the limited sense of a boy or young servant. **uppan blancan**: "upon a [white] horse." **iċ stifle**: "I am become rigid." **wit**: "we two." **ġewæpnod 7 ġesierwed**: **armed & armoured**: "weaponed and equipped." **hiera þone fulostan**: "of them the foulest.

Robert Duncan: Often I Am Permitted to Return to a Meadow
wafung: **scene**: from *wafian*, to "wonder at." **ġetimbrunga**: **architectures**: from *timbrian*, to "build" or "construct." **ġedryhta**: **hosts**: that is, troops of retainers. **drefung**: **disturbance**: from *drefan*, to "trouble." **efne swefn**: **only a dream**: in OE, *dream* means "joy" and "merriment." **toġeanes þære sunnan frumstowe**:

"toward the sun's place of origin." **niþerstiġe**: "descent."
dieġelnesse: **secret. staþolæht**: given property: that is,
real possessions, an estate. **wiþ dwolman**: **against cha-
os**: from *dwolian*, to "err" or "stray." **eċe wyrdtacen**:
everlasting omen: although the combination *æfre + læs-
tende* is theoretically possible in OE, it is not recorded.
wyrdtacen: "weird token."

H.D.: Storm
This poem serves as a caveat against an easy correla-
tion between historical "purity" of speech and modern-
ist (in this case, imagist) "purity" of direct expression.
Most of H.D.'s strong verb forms here are not derived
from OE roots but from words that came into the lan-
guage during the Middle English and Early Modern pe-
riods: "crack" from Old High German, "crushed" from
Old French, "split" from Middle Dutch, "swirl" from
Old Norse, "crash" and "hurled" from English's natural
capacity for inventive word-formation. The OE words
in the back-translation have approximate meanings at
best—**Þu bricst:** thou breakest; **þu clyfst:** thou cleavest;
gebriesed: bruised; **rended:** rent; **þu hwærfiast:** thou
revolvest.

James Laughlin: It Does Me Good
ortġeardwearda an: "of the orchardwarders one." **be
ġeonglingum**: **by boys**: The word "boy" and its alterna-
tive "lad" are Middle English and of unknown origin.
The word "smile," also, first appeared in ME, but de-

91

rived from a Germanic root common to many languages. Thus, **smile at me** becomes **hliehhan on me**: "laugh [i.e., pleasantly] on me." **min eaþmodnes self heo ricsaþ**: "my humility herself she rules."

Denise Levertov: Illustrious Ancestors
Se Rabbi: "The Rabbi"—as in the OE Gospel of St. John. The word *rav*, meaning in Hebrew "great one," originally the title of respect for Talmudic scholars in the late Babylonian Jewish community, was adopted by the Hasidim of Eastern Europe for their wise men and community leaders. The more commonly known term *rabbi* was the Palestinian equivalent of *rav* and means, simply, "my great one." **nolde**: *ne wolde*, that is, "did not wish." **man funde**: **it was found**: "one found." Similarly, **swa man sæġþ**: **as it is said**. **to sciepenne,/ ...sċopleoþ**: **to make,/ ... poems**: "to shape [create]/ ...poet-songs." OE *sċop* means "poet." **ġerynelicu**: **mysterious**: from OE *run*, "rune."

Robert Lowell: Water
unc: "us two"—a dual construction. **sticcaliċan/ ġewindu**: "sticklike windings." **to æse**: **for bait**: cf. Dutch *aas*. **wæron grinode**: **were trapped**: from *grin-ian*, to "ensnare." The word *træppe* in OE existed only as a noun. **Wit**: "we two." **uppan smeþum stanstyċċe**: "upon a smooth piece of stone." **þæs hiwes/sċire blostmena**: "of the color of bright flowers." The word "iris," Greek derived, came into English rather late. **awasċed...**

awasċede: instead of **drenched**, which in OE had the restricted sense of "causing to drink." **uncerum fotum**: "feet of us two." **meremægden**: an obvious combination but not found until the fourteenth century. OE, however, does have *merewif*. **muscellan**: "mussels." The word "barnacle," very likely of Celtic origin, is a Middle English word.

Michael McClure: Two Haiku
Smitt: "smiteth." The root *smack* has a long history in all Germanic languages but in English doesn't take on the meaning of "hitting" until the nineteenth century. **HARA:** "hare." The word "rabbit" is early Modern English, apparently derived from Old North French.

Marianne Moore: Poetry
mid fullfremedre forghogodnesse: **with a perfect contempt**: cf. the German *Verhöhnung*.

Marianne Moore: To a Steam Roller
STEAMTREDERE: "steamtrampler." **Seo sweotolung**: **The Illustration**: that is, "manifestation" or "explanation," from the verb, *sweotolian*. **brycas**: "fragments," from *brecan*, to "break." "Chip" in OE—*ċipp*—means "cut log" or "beam." **to þære grundstowe þæs cennendes cludes**: "to the ground-place of the birthing rock." **Were not "impersonal judgment in aesthetic / matters, a metaphysical impossibility"** is almost beyond the expressive capabilities of OE as it has come

down to us. **Were not**: **Ġif nære**: "If n[ot]-were." **impersonal judgment**: **unagen dom**: "not-one's-own doom." **in aesthetic / matters**: **be andġietsumum / intingum**: *andġiet* means "sense," "intelligence," "understanding"; *-sum* is an adjectival suffix; *intinga*, "in-thing." **uþwitalicu**: "philosophical," "out-wit-ly." **unmihtnes**: from *unmiht*, "impossible" ("un-might"), with the noun suffix *-nes*. **ġerisnesse**: from *ġerisan*, "befit."

Marianne Moore: O to Be a Dragon
seolcwyrmes / ġemet oþþe unmæte: **of silkworm / size or immense**: both *ġemet* and *unmæte* are related to the verb *metan*, to "measure." Cf. Wallace Stevens, "Anecdote of the Jar" ("Þæs Crocces Spell"), l. 8.

Toby Olson: The Spot
of his hlæfdiġan gydenne: "of his lady a goddess." In OE, *wif* is grammatically of neutral gender—an "it" (*hit*) not a "her" (*hiere*)—which destroys the sense of the poem. **ġeswæpa**: "sweepings." **hiere wammas**: "her blemishes." **lendenu**: "loins." **wamlease 7 ġestenċe**: "blemishless and fragrant." **huniġteare**: **nectar**: "honey-tear." **bleġene**: "blain." **inþicgan**: "in-take." **stenċ**: **smell**: either pleasant or unpleasant. Cf. the adjective **ġestenċe** above. **on þæm hiwum weallweorca**: "in the forms of wall-masonry." **on þære wambum**: **in the bellies**: OE *wamb*, "stomach," became the modern "womb."

George Oppen: Boy's Room
ĠEONGLINGES BUR: "YOUNGLING'S BOWER."
wene.... / Wenunga: **suppose....** / **Perhaps**: both words
have the root sense of hope/thought/expectation. **myne-
tere**: **banker**: a "moneychanger" or "minter."

Ezra Pound: A Girl
hæwene blostmas: "purple/blue flowers." The OE word
for *Viola odorata*, whatever it may have been, was re-
placed by the Old French *violete*.

Ezra Pound: In a Station of the Metro
METRO: from *chemin de fer métropolitain*, deriving
from the Greek for "mother-" or "womb-city" (in OE,
moder, *wamb*). "In a Station of the Metro" is among the
"purist" of Imagist poems. Yet the self-conscious phras-
ing of the first line, its key word **apparition** so clearly
"un-English," hints that it was the second, more thor-
oughly "Saxon" line which may have come full-blown
to Pound, even if he did, as he later explained, pare the
poem down from thirty to two lines.

Ezra Pound: The River-Merchant's Wife: A Letter
uppan bambusum palum: **on bamboo stilts**: the word
"bamboo" is ultimately Malaysian, but its Neo-Latin
form, *bambusa*, lends itself easily to OE inflection. As
for "stilts," I am inclined to think there existed an OE
word on the order of *stilta*. Middle English has *stilte*,
while most other Germanic languages have analogous

forms, and all are derived from the same, albeit conjectural, root. But in the absence of clear evidence, "poles" seems the best choice here. **Þu eodest**: "Thou walked." The OE verb *wealcian* means to "toss" or "roll." **sess**: **seat**: OE *set* and *setl* refer mainly to a place of settlement (but note *weardsetl*: **look out**, or "guard place" below). **Clipod**: **Called to**: The verb *ċeallian* appears only once in OE records, in the narrow sense of "shout." **Iċ blann fram gramum andwlitan**: "I ceased from angry faces." **Hie hefiġaþ me**: "They lie heavy on me."

John Ratti: Album

ĠEMYNDBOC: that is, "MEMORY BOOK." The word "album," meaning a blank or "white" (Latin, *albus*) book, is modern. **ġelic cytelingum**: **like kittens**: "kitlings." "Kitten" is a Middle English word, derived from French. The word *cyteling*, however, is conjectural, though *catt* is not; here no doubt a native word must have been lost. **muþas samodfæste mid hocum**: "mouths together-fastened with hooks." **ætiewede**: **displayed**: from *ætiewan*, a verb combination of *æt* ("at") and *eage* ("eye"). **cneowehtum / wuda horde**: "knotty / board of wood." **teah upp his breċ**: "tugged up his breeches." **treowa fleot**: "float of trees." **wæs folod**: **was foaled**: by analogy with modern Dutch and German *veulenen* and *fohlen*. OE has *fola*, "foal," and *ġefola*, "with foal," but the verb only first appears in Middle English.

96

Kenneth Rexroth: Delia Rexroth

Slæpiġne: the accusative case. *Slæpiġ* is not recorded in OE, but *unslæpiġ*, "sleepless," is. **þa enta ġeweorc**: "the work of giants," a frequent OE phrase for ancient ruins (cf. *The Wanderer*, l. 87). The word "pyramid" is not recorded until the fourteenth century. It is derived from the Greco-Latin *pyramis* and is of uncertain meaning and origin. **stod**: **has cost**: "has stood." **fæhunga**: **paintings**: from *fæhan*, to "paint." **Þa dieran wyrde**: **The precious consequences**: "the dear fates."

Jerome Rothenberg: A Poem in Yellow after Tristan Tzara

sacc: The word "basket" is of uncertain origin and comes into the language in the thirteenth century. Here is a clear case in which the native word for an everyday object must have been replaced. **langaþ hit**: "longs for it." The OE verb to "crave," *crafian*, has a narrow, legalistic sense of demanding justice.

Gary Snyder: By Frazier Creek Falls

healf-wudufæstede: **half-forested**: "half-woodfast," derived from *wundufæsten*, meaning "forest covering," "forest stronghold," or in poetical metaphor, "ship." **sinewealtu**: **round**: It is interesting that the Old French *rond-* displaced what must have been common expressions of native stock denoting roundness in all Germanic languages. See the note below to Wallace Stevens, "The Anecdote of the Jar." **swogendu cwaciendu**:

rustling trembling: "soughing quaking."

Wallace Stevens: Anecdote of the Jar
sinewealt: **round**: with the implied root meaning of unsteadiness, like a quivering bag of water. See the note above to Gary Snyder, "By Frazier Creek Falls." **ne... naeniġne... ne**: emphatic triple negative, "He no gave (no)any bird nor bush."

Wallace Stevens: The Glass of Water
glæsfæt: "glassvat." **Maniġra an**: "of many one," a partitive genitive construction. **On þæm ġeondcyndliċum**: **In the metaphysical**: from *cyndliċ*, "natural." **famiġan ċeaflas**: **frothy jaws**: "foamy jowls." **brytsenna**: "fragments." **þa ġesceapbæran partas of leoþum**: **the plastic parts of poems**: *ġesceapbære*, the uninflected form of the word, carries the sense of "shapable"; *part*, a Latin borrowing, referred in King Alfred's time especially to a part of speech. **Hlynsiaþ**: "Resound." **cariende**: **worrying**: "caring." The verb *wyrġan* is limited in meaning to causing death by strangulation. **cartan**: in a strict sense, *cartan* are not really gaming cards but pieces of paper or documents. The earliest use of "cards" to refer to apparatus for amusement is in the fourteenth century.

Wallace Stevens: The Motive for Metaphor
SE INTINGA FOR ĠEONDLÆDUNGE: THE MOTIVE FOR METAPHOR: "THE CAUSE [REASON] FOR BEYOND-CARRYING." **Þæm heofone**

beorhtran lyt: **The slightly brighter sky**: "The heaven brighter by a little."

William Carlos Williams: The Widow's Lament in Springtime
Of all the poems in this collection, those by Williams translate most readily into OE. This raises some interesting thoughts about the "purity," and by extension the clarity, of his American speech.

William Carlos Williams: The Red Wheelbarrow
See note above to "The Widow's Lament in Springtime."

William Carlos Williams: This Is Just to Say
isċieste: "icechest." The combination *isbox* in OE is meaningless, since the second element refers only to boxwood and the boxtree. **smæccliċe**: **delicious**: as in Dutch (*smakelijk*).

ACKNOWLEDGMENTS

100

GREEN INTEGER
Pataphysics and Pedantry
Douglas Messerli, *Publisher*

Essays, Manifestos, Statements, Speeches, Maxims,
Epistles, Diaristic Notes, Narrative, Natural Histories,
Poems, Plays, Performances, Ramblings, Revelations
and all such ephemera as may appear necessary
to bring society into a slight tremolo of confusion
and fright at least.

Individuals may order Green Integer titles through PayPal
www.paypal.com
Please pay the price listed below plus $2.00 for postage to Green
Integer through the PayPal system. You can also visit our site at
www.greeninteger.com
If you have questions please feel free to e-mail the publisher at
douglasmesserli@gmail.com
Bookstores and libraries should order through our distributors
USA and Canada: Consortium Book Sales
and Distribution/Perseus Books
United Kingdom and Europe: Turnaround Publisher Services
Unit 3, Olympia Trading Estate, Coburg Road, Wood Green,
London N22 6TZ UK

*

SELECTED BOOKS OF POETRY

Adonis *If Only the Sea Could Sleep: Love Poems* [1-931243-29-8]
$11.95
Thérèse Bachand *luce a cavallo* [978-1-933382-31-9] $12.95
Charles Bernstein *Republics of Reality: 1975-1995* [Sun & Moon
Press: 1-55713-304-2] $14.95
Shadowtime [978-1-933382-00-5] $11.95

Oswald Egger *Room of Rumor: Tunings* [978-1-931243-66-7] $9.95

Paul Éluard *A Moral Lesson* [978-1-931243-95-7] $10.95

Nikos Engonopoulos *Acropolis and Tram: Poems 1938-1978* [978-1-933382-37-1] $13.95

Federico García Lorca *Suites* [1-892295-61-X] $12.95

Dieter M. Gräf *Tousled Beauty* [978-1-933382-01-2] $11.95
Tussi Research [978-1-933382-86-9] $13.96

Hagiwara Sakutarō *Howling at the Moon: Poems and Prose* [1-931243-01-8] $11.95

Hsi Muren *Across the Darkness of the River* [1-931243-24-7] $9.95

Hsu Hui-chih *Book of Reincarnation* [1-931243-32-8] $9.95

Ko Un *Himalaya Poems* [978-1-55713-412-7] $13.95
Songs for Tomorrow: Poems 1961-2001 [978-1-933382-70-8] $15.95
Ten Thousand Lives [978-1-933382-06-7] $14.95

Friederike Mayröcker *with each clouded peak* [Sun & Moon Press: 1-55713-277-1] $11.95

Deborah Meadows *Representing Absence* [978-1-931243-77-3] $9.95
Thin Gloves [978-1-933382-19-7] $12.95

Douglas Messerli *After* [Sun & Moon Press: 1-55713-353-0] $10.95
Bow Down [ML&NLF: 1-928801-04-8] $12.95
First Words [978-1-931243-41-4] $10.95
ed. *Listen to the Mockingbird: American Folksongs and Popular Music Lyrics of the 19th Century* [978-1-892295-20-0] $13.95
Maxims from My Mother's Milk/Hymns to Him: A Dialogue [Sun & Moon Press: 1-55713-047-7] $8.95

Vítězslav Nezval •*Antilyrik & Other Poems* [1-892295-75-X] $10.95

Henrik Nordbrandt *The Hangman's Lament: Poems* [978-1-931243-56-8] $10.95

Antonio Porta *Metropolis* [1-892295-12-1] $10.95

Stephen Ratcliffe *Sound / (system)* [1-931243-35-2] $12.95

Elizabeth Robinson *Pure Descent* [Sun & Moon Press: 1-55713-410-3] $10.95

Reina María Rodríguez *Violet Island and Other Poems* [978-1-892295-65-1] $12.95

Gonzalo Rojas *From the Lightning: Selected Poems* [978-1-933382-64-7] $14.95

Jean-Pierre Rosnay *When a Poet Sees a Chestnut Tree* [978-1-933382-20-3] $12.95

Joe Ross *EQUATIONS=equals* [978-1-931243-61-2] $10.95
  Wordlick [978-1-55713-415-8] $11.95

Paul Snoek *Hercules Richelieu* and *Nostradamus* [1-892295-42-3] $10.95

  The Song of Songs: Shir Hashirim [1-931243-05-0] $9.95

Adriano Spatola *The Position of Things: Collected Poems 1961-1992* [978-1-933382-45-6] $15.95

Takamura Kōtarō *The Chieko Poems* [978-1-933382-75-3] $12.95

Tomas Tranströmer *The Sorrow Gondola* [978-1-933382-44-9] $11.95

Yang Lian *Yi* [1-892295-68-7] $14.95

Visar Zhiti *The Condemned Apple: Selected Poetry* [978-1-931243-72-8] $10.95